Manners
on the
School Bus

by Amanda Doering Tourville   illustrated by Chris Lensch

PICTURE WINDOW BOOKS
Minneapolis, Minnesota

Special thanks to our advisers for their expertise:

Kay A. Augustine, Ed.S.
National Character Development Consultant and Trainer
West Des Moines, Iowa

Terry Flaherty, Ph.D., Professor of English
Minnesota State University, Mankato

Editor: Shelly Lyons
Designer: Tracy Davies
Page Production: Melissa Kes
Art Director: Nathan Gassman
Editorial Director: Nick Healy
The illustrations in this book were created digitally.

Picture Window Books
1710 Roe Crest Drive
North Mankato, MN 56003
www.picturewindowbooks.com

Library of Congress Cataloging-in-Publication Data
Tourville, Amanda Doering, 1980-
Manners on the school bus / by Amanda Doering Tourville ;
illustrated by Chris Lensch.
p. cm. — (Way to Be!)
Includes index.
ISBN 978-1-4048-5311-9 (library binding)
ISBN 978-1-4048-5312-6 (paperback)
1. Travel etiquette—Juvenile literature. 2. School buses—Juvenile literature.
I. Lensch, Chris. II. Title.
BJ2140.T68 2009
395.5—dc22   2008039133

Lots of kids ride a school bus to school. Using good manners on the bus means everyone can have a nice trip. Good manners help keep you safe, too.

There are lots of ways you can use good manners on the school bus.

Dion is always on time for the school bus. He doesn't make the driver wait.

He is using good manners.

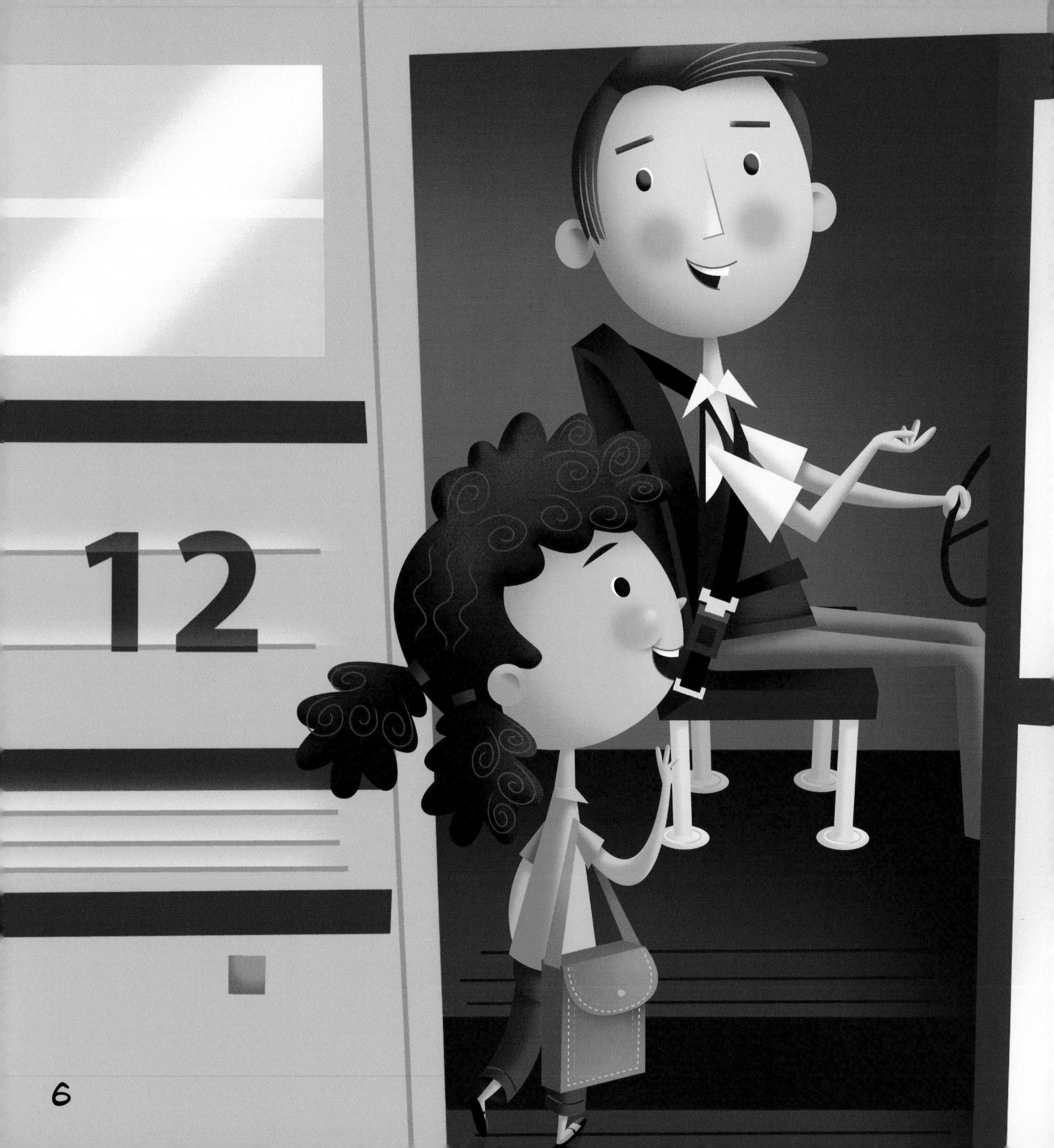
12

Eliza climbs up the bus stairs. She smiles at the driver and says, "Good morning."

She is using good manners.

James and Connor face forward in their seats. They talk quietly to each other.

They are using good manners.

Alicia gets on the bus. She waits patiently until the person ahead of her sits down.

Alicia is using good manners.

"May I sit by you?" a boy asks Carter.
Carter smiles and nods his head.

Carter is using good manners.

Mia and Karin keep their hands to themselves. They keep their feet and book bags out of the aisles.

They are using good manners.

Tyrell and Sarah are the oldest kids on the bus. They are nice to the younger kids. They don't tease or bother them.

Tyrell and Sarah are using good manners.

Josh waits his turn to get off the bus. He never pushes the people in front of him.

He is using good manners.

"Thanks for the ride," Megan tells the bus driver. "Have a nice day!"

She is using good manners.

It is important to use good manners on the school bus. Good manners make a nice, safe ride for everyone.

Fun Facts

Some children who live in rural areas may ride the bus for two hours each day.

Most kids in South Korea walk or take public buses to school.

Students in the United States used to ride in "school hacks," or horse-drawn carriages.

In some countries, families must pay for their children to ride the school bus.

School buses in Canada are yellow, too.

In the United States, about 25 million students ride the bus to school.

To Learn More

More Books to Read

Bailey, Suzanne E. *Manners Are Cool.* Anaheim, Calif.:
    Creative Continuum, Inc., 2005.
Mattern, Joanne. *Staying Safe on the School Bus.* Milwaukee:
    Weekly Reader Early Learning Library, 2007.
Thomas, Pat. *My Manners Matter: A First Look at Being Polite.*
    New York: Barron's, 2006.

On the Web

FactHound offers a safe, fun way to find educator-approved
Internet sites related to this book.

Here's what you do:
1. Visit *www.facthound.com*
2. Choose your grade level.
3. Begin your search.

This book's ID number is 9781404853119

Look for all of the books in the Way to Be! Manners series:

Manners at a Friend's House

Manners at School

Manners at the Table

Manners in Public

Manners in the Library

Manners in the Lunchroom

Manners on the Playground

Manners on the School Bus

Manners on the Telephone

Manners with a Library Book

Index